PREFAB HOME

MICHAEL BUCHANAN

PHOTOGRAPHS BY
FRANKLIN AND ESTHER SCHMIDT

Gibbs Smith, Publisher
Salt Lake City

First Edition

08 07 06 05 04   5 4 3 2 1

Published by

Gibbs Smith, Publisher

P.O. Box 667

Layton, Utah 84041

Orders: 1.800.748.5439

www.gibbs-smith.com

Designed by Debra McQuiston

Printed and bound in Hong Kong

Library of Congress Control Number: 2004107690

ISBN 1-58685-350-3

For my mother, whose love and support—here on earth and from the heavens—sustains all my dreams.

CONTENTS

FOREWORD	**vii**
ACKNOWLEDGMENTS	**xi**
INTRODUCTION	**13**
CHAPTER 1 History of Modular Construction	**21**
CHAPTER 2 The Language of Modular Construction	**37**
CHAPTER 3 Design Recipe for a Modular Bungalow	**69**
CHAPTER 4 Updating Arts and Crafts Detail	**95**
CHAPTER 5 Creating the Look for Less	**125**
CONCLUSION	**143**
RESOURCES	**158**

FOREWORD

Chadsworth columns
placed on stone-clad
pillars with pergola
above create a grace-
ful front porch seating
area—a perfect place
to enjoy spring days
and summer evenings.

In this book, Michael Buchanan takes readers on a journey to the edges of the known universe of home design. He presents as a case study his own experiences in creating a showplace custom home using mostly mid-range, off-the-shelf components in a house assembled from prefabricated modular components.

Buchanan invites the reader into the process, exploring his starting assumptions, allowing the reader to examine the project as it unfolded and consider where those preconceptions led. He frankly discusses his mistakes as well as his successes in a way that makes reading this book a much-less-expensive vicarious learning experience.

As a builder, remodeler, and custom furniture and cabinetmaker for more than twenty years, I know the scope of the task he set himself. I respect the candor with which he enumerates the frustrations and obstacles he encountered and the compromises he found himself deciding to make along the way.

This is no fairy tale. It is the story of a complex, multifaceted project—a creative and ultimately rewarding struggle towards the realization of a dream. But it is exceptionally straightforward—and therefore unusually useful—in assessing the differences between the dream and the reality and describing how the first becomes the second.

Buchanan explains how he applies his "good-better-best" approach to design on a budget. A baseline of good—but not "deluxe"—quality is established for most of the construction. This keeps basic costs down. The money saved is then applied to providing a "better" level of quality in those areas where it will be most appreciated. These areas can then be accented with a few "best" touches, accents that add real originality and personality to the design.

He discusses how to apply design sensibility to the modular "blocks" of prefabricated construction and how detailing can create an identity for a building. He demonstrates how, by placing the building in the landscape in a thoughtful way, by off-setting components to create interesting rooflines and wall angles, by employing a variety of exterior finish materials to create textural interest (and in many other small but crucial ways), one can reinvent modular construction to one's own taste while saving money on construction costs.

As Buchanan himself suggests, the idea of modular, or prefabricated, construction has taken on negative connotations in recent decades. Having worked on some of the beautifully made early Arts and Crafts kit houses manufactured in the first decades of the twentieth century, I know this does not have to be so. Given the cost savings inherent in the construction technique, a prefabricated shell will generally be less expensive than a site-built structure of exactly the same specifications, configuration, and quality.

Buchanan suggests that working with home manufacturers, taking advantage of their labor-efficient methods and the price advantages of bulk purchasing, one can save substantial amounts of money that can then be invested in the most important aspects of the building. His own experience, the fits and starts of his learning curve notwithstanding, bears him out, and lays out a useful set of parameters that others can profitably follow in attempting to emulate—and even improve on—his efforts.

—Ned Depew
Author, home inspector, and
NPR radio commentator

The finished exterior features a blending of materials, styles, and textures, all meant to give the appearance of a house that has been changed over the years. Landscaping includes an English-edge sea-pebble drive with specimen trees, ferns, and hand-crafted window boxes.

ACKNOWLEDGMENTS

My vision was nurtured and strengthened by many, and I am grateful. I could not have persevered with this adventure without the enduring love and faithful companionship of Gary and Miss Patty. Tim Langan, architect extraordinaire, focused on the details and turned my daydreams into reality. Rose Meecham attended to getting the project off the ground. Marie Kameen pulled it all together, amazing me with her many wonderful talents. And finally, my family offered approval and assurance that I was on the right path, yet never let me forget who I am or where I came from. Thank you, all.

(**Left**) A side entrance into the master bedroom wing shows different siding materials used to convey the feeling that the house has been added onto through the years. (**Opposite Page**) The hallway to the master bedroom wing with factory-installed cabinets will take on a whole new look once the decorator touches have been added.

INTRODUCTION

ine is a longing shared by all creatures, great and small: to build a house. Whether I peer into the abandoned bird's nest left above my kitchen arbor or reflect on the complexities of twenty-first-century American life, I know that creating a dwelling is an ageless and universal dream. We may imagine a modest, functional home or a customized, luxurious space: our vision begins to take shape, and then we move to the often complex and usually expensive reality of giving form to our dreams.

My own passion for building a house seems a natural enough outgrowth of the many years I have spent in the design business. I have had a wonderful education on what makes a house and design successful. Common sense tells us that as a home is improved its value increases; but my own experience has been that it is more than simple upgrades that add value to a house.

As I worked to incorporate classic European design aesthetics, I found that the value of even the simplest properties increased beyond the expectations of both my clients and real estate brokers. I watched the worth of modest dwellings significantly increase as a result of my efforts and soon realized two things about my creative instincts: I was delighted that my work was so well received, and then I knew it was time to use those instincts from the ground up.

I felt confident that the design would be pleasing to the current real estate market, but I wondered if I could pursue the dream on a realistic budget, without sacrificing my sense of style—and perhaps even make a profit at it.

My passion for both real estate and the design business led me to take the risk. If this project is anything like the financial gamble I took in the stock market, I will be living in the poorhouse; however, I believe I can produce a successful design that will lead to financial gain. The goal, of course, in any speculative project is to minimize costs. Anyone who has moved from turning a dream into reality knows all too well that keeping costs down is one of the

biggest challenges. While you are in the design phase, there is no money attached to your wonderful design revelations. But a jolt of reality hits when the budget numbers come in, and immediately cuts must be made.

The cut that will have the most impact on the cost is the overall size of the house. When designing, the bigger the better is okay if money is no object. But once again, the reality may call for a reassessment of room sizes. If you look at your family size and lifestyle, you may find that there is extra breathing room that can be pared down without compromising comfort.

The years I have spent in the design and construction industry have given me an in-depth knowledge of the cost of construction per foot when using conventional building methods. To get an idea on square-foot pricing, keep in mind that there is a huge range in cost depending on location, cost of materials and labor, etc. Prices can range from a low of $85 per square foot to $125–$150 for the average level of finish and detail,

(Left) A view of the unfinished living room area shortly after delivery. (Opposite Page) A close-up view of the second-floor landing with a glimpse into the guest bathroom.

(Opposite Page) The guest bathroom features metro tiles that were popular at the turn of the century and hand-printed Sanderson & Sons wallpaper in a light and airy lilac floral pattern.
(Right) All the fixtures in the powder room on the first floor were installed at the factory. Products are Kohler and were chosen for their elegant style. The interesting floor tile mosaic was found by the designer at an antiques store and installed at the factory. It's a good example of how easily modular construction can be customized.

and to $225–$250 for a nicely appointed home. For the top-notch level of finish and detail, one could expect to pay $500–$1,000 per square foot, depending on materials used.

A budget can be quickly established by taking the overall square footage of the house and multiplying by the number that reflects the level of finish desired. As I began this project, I knew that the level of finish I was striving for would be in the $250–$500 range; however, I needed to find a way to cut that number in half.

Sounds like a tall order, but as I researched various building options, I determined that prefabricated construction would be the most cost-efficient choice. The ideal budget could be met with prefab (modular) construction, and so it was that I began the pursuit of my dream—first looking back at the turn-of-the-century catalog bungalows and then looking forward to the technology that would allow me to afford all the bells and whistles of my dream.

Perhaps my earliest hurdle was

to rescue the modular home from its own reputation: too often it is thought of as a sterile, boring, double-wide; and unfortunately those attributes were often mentioned as I discussed this project. I knew that to dispel this notion, I would not only have to call upon the rich diversity of American design but also peer into the melting pot. The colorful blend of cultural influences of our immigrant ancestors would color my twenty-first-century bungalow; and while the

simplicity of its design would be true to its heritage, I would clothe it in the elegance of the Old World. Creating a shelter of grace and beauty aroused my interest and intentions, but perhaps another goal was to have this question posed by those who came upon my bungalow: "This is a modular?"

A recent CNN/Money report may have summed it up best: ". . . put the words 'prefab' and 'home' together and we cringe." Harvard Housing Studies scholar William Apgar makes two important observations on this notion: prefab may have earned its "bad name" because so many are built to "lower standards," but even though it has been pigeonholed as "low-end, . . . nothing says it can't be high end." (Max, Sarah, "Prefab Chic," CNNMoney.com, August 14, 2003.)

Reaching for the high end was not without frustration and compromise, but my dream was sustained and driven by the passion I felt for the project. I hope this how-to will not only inspire but also help others over some of these hurdles. For whether I worked through simple stumbling blocks or giant brick walls, I never lost sight of my bungalow, a petite castle nestled in the New England hills.

Michael Buchanan

CHAPTER 1

"WE WANT THE ENDURING QUALITY
OF CLASSIC DESIGN AND ECLECTIC APPOINTMENTS—
A PLACE TO RAISE OUR FAMILIES AND FIND SANCTUARY
FROM THE COMPLEXITIES OF OUR LIVES."

HISTORY OF MODULAR CONSTRUCTION

With the center modular unit in place, the sunroom wing is in the air and ready to be set down beside it to form a right-side wing.

Giving shape and substance to a dream requires some homework. In this case it was an exploration of the cultural influences and values that created common themes in our architectural history, including a survey of housing design and modular construction.

As the curtain was falling on the Gilded Age and America entered the twentieth century, the explosion of industry, westward expansion, and a new wave of cheap immigrant labor led to unheard-of prosperity among the crowns of industry. The newly wealthy celebrated their success as never before: ostentatious and extravagant living announced their status, while more Americans than ever before toiled in the gloom of poverty. A new yearning for the values that had led to our greatness was born of their labors—for even as the blue bloods made way for the newly prosperous, the vast majority of us comprised a hard-working middle class with simple needs and common dreams.

The new American design rebelled against the excesses of its recent past and returned to the simplicity of its pioneer roots. Encouraged by the philosophy of the Progressive Era, which espoused

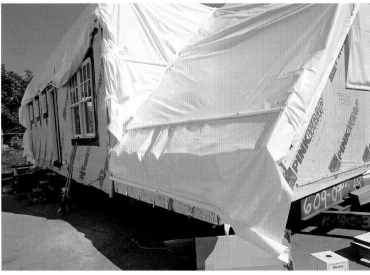

social justice and economic opportunity for all, and sustained by the Arts and Crafts movement, the bungalow became the new American housing icon. Both practical and affordable, the simple design of the bungalow allowed for individual style and for incorporating natural materials and artistic elements. Cluttered interiors were soon replaced by open living areas and built-in furniture, not to mention such conveniences as indoor plumbing.

Of course there were variations in the style of the bungalow; as with all things American, each region put its own stamp on the design, and individual builders and homeowners imposed their specifications. And yet there were common features: low-pitched roofs, simple lines, large porches, and exposed roof rafters on the outside and charming nooks and crannies around an open floor plan on the inside. What contributed to the popularity of this simple home design? Perhaps purely its affordability; but maybe it was that its rustic cottage feeling invoked the sentiment conveyed by the popular embroidered sampler of the time, "Be it ever so humble, there's no place like home."

With the simplification of home design came the catalog houses, the mail-order kits that became the rage of the expanding middle class. They

(Opposite Page)
Views of the second-
floor unit as it hovers
midair and a crane
operator slowly
moves it into place
atop the main first-
floor unit.
(Right) A cable/latch
system is used to
secure the unit to the
crane for safe move-
ment and placement.

started small and were initially meant to be only summer vacation homes; but in 1910 Aladdin Homes of Bay City, Michigan, took the concept to a whole new level. They were followed by the well-known Sears, Roebuck and Company houses (and several others), and a look at the catalogs furnished to interested buyers conveys the story in its own words.

The opening pages of most of the catalogs focused on the science and technology that had led to the development of homes by mail. It was necessary to convince potential buyers that such prefabrication was not only economical but also safe and sound. One catalog, Bennett Homes,

called their models "Better Built Ready-Cut" and proclaimed that science had solved the "high cost of home-building." Aladdin offered a "dollar a knot guarantee" on their "Readi-Cut" homes; they stated that the U.S. government had granted them exclusive use of their tagline, "Sold by the Golden Rule." Sears, Roebuck and Company labeled their models "Honor-Bilt Modern Homes," promising to help America meet the demand for "substantial and modern homes for its industrial and thrifty people."

No matter the language of their sales pitch, each of the companies agreed that labor-saving machine

(**Left**) A close-up of the crane as it moves into place to lift a module and set it in place.
(**Above**) The sloping roof section is hoisted from a delivery truck for placement.

construction, standardization of lumber size and length, bulk purchasing, and quantity production of millwork would make housing affordable for the masses. And, yet, with all of their standardization, the catalog companies offered a pretty good assortment of styles and design. Although they were all grouped under the label of "bungalows," styles included the two-story center hall colonial, the ever-popular Cape Cod, the gambrel-roof Dutch farmhouse, the stylish and detailed Queen Anne, and even the stucco-finished Spanish-mission style.

In addition to having a choice of style and design, each offering came with an options list, and these included paint color, wood type, masonry work, and door and cabinet design, among others. Add-ons were also available: Sears offered sun porches, and Aladdin offered enclosed rear entrances with cellar stairs. The car was still called an automobile and though it was not in widespread use, each of the companies offered free-standing garages—some designed to be just large enough to "admit a Ford touring car with top either up or down."

Each of the companies had one final ace up their sleeve: time! Aladdin used it best by titling its 1917 catalog

the "Built in a Day" House Catalog. Most of the house kits were shipped by rail; usually two boxcars were needed for the whole deal. Often the pieces were sent in staggered shipments to allow for completion of the project in stages. In its catalog, Sears estimated the carpenter labor hours at about 350 for their "Honor-Bilt" systems, as opposed to about 585 for stick construction. And while 350 hours is a long way from "built in a day," Sears did offer sectional summer cottages that could, indeed, be assembled in about eight hours.

The housing boom was on and continued even through the early depression years before finally slowing

as a recovering economy eventually gave way to World War II. Returning GIs looked to meet their housing needs with such mass-produced homes as the Levittowners. The brainchild of builder, developer, and marketing genius Bill Levitt began along the overcrowded Northeast corridor as Levitt created first his suburb on Long Island and then one in Pennsylvania and another in New Jersey. In 1951, as he unveiled plans for building more than 17,000 houses between Routes 1 and 13, he launched a promotional campaign that he dubbed "democracy in real estate," reiterating the connection between homeownership and the American dream.

Levitt's version of mass-produced housing was in many ways similar to the building efficiency of modular construction, but all the work was completed assembly-line style on-site. Construction crews arrived with special skills and special tasks; like mailmen on their appointed rounds, they completed their specific functions and moved to the house next door. With simple designs—primarily

(**Above Left**) The interior of a modular unit that will become a utility/laundry area and form the hallway that leads to the master bedroom wing. (**Right**) The second floor is being moved into place as the set crew approaches to insure that placement is successfully aligned.

MODULAR MINUTIAE: PAST

· The first American modular was shipped from England in the 1600s
· Settlers bound for the heartland took modular housing with them in the 1800s
· Eminent architects explored the use of modular construction in the early 1900s
· Catalog houses filled the need for affordable housing in the mid-1900s
· Postwar housing needs saw builders try to emulate the auto industry assembly line
· Trailer coaches made their debut for American travelers in the 1920s

(Source: **Pre-Fab,** by Allison Arieff and Bryan Burkhart, Gibbs Smith, Publisher, 2002)

single-story ranches—the houses went up at the rate of about thirty-five to forty per day; "little boxes made of ticky-tacky," sang Pete Seeger.

Unlike the simple bungalow design that was charming and cozy and achieved both affordability and individuality, the cookie-cutter Levittowners often left even their owners lost along a lane of look-alikes. Urban blight followed this mass exodus of the middle class, and this was also intensified by the pace of the times. Factories were at full production as demand for cars, appliances, televisions, and all those symbols of the American dream were made available to a more solvent and upwardly mobile citizenry. Highways, bridges, airports, and skyscrapers

(**Left**) Deck railing from Weyerhaeuser. The ChoiceDeck system is a composite deck and railing system that is made from recycled plastic and wood elements.
(**Right**) A factory worker adds finishing touches to hardwood flooring. Even in the eleventh hour, as the unit is readied for shipping, a quality-control issue is addressed before final packing.

(Left) A set-crew worker walks along the foundation edge as the first-floor unit is moved into place. (Right) Foundation and sand/grading that will be backfilled when the house is set and installation of the plumbing and septic are complete.

dominated the building trades, and suddenly more homeowners became do-it-yourselfers. They looked to themselves to personalize and redesign their homes.

The later decades of the century were a time for gentrification, restoration, renovation, and moving toward improving the aesthetics not only of our residential neighborhoods but our cities as well. As the baby boomers became home buyers, a generation that had grown up in those "little boxes" seemed to crave just what the early proponents of the Arts and Crafts movement wanted:

better design, more natural elements, and a home that reflected their individuality.

The new millennium, then, finds us once again looking at bungalows, modular construction, harmony with our surroundings, and the simple comforts that were the hallmark of the Arts and Crafts era. We want the enduring quality of classic design and eclectic appointments—a place to raise our families and find sanctuary from the complexities of our twenty-first-century lives.

CHAPTER 2

" UNLIKE SITE-BUILT HOMES,
WHICH BEGIN WITH EXTERIOR FRAMING AND ROOFING,
MODULAR HOMES ARE BUILT FROM THE INSIDE OUT. "

THE LANGUAGE OF MODULAR CONSTRUCTION

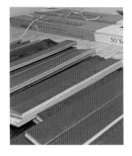    

(**Left**) Rear exterior view shows that the roof modular unit has now been placed atop the main unit.

f imagination led to exploration, then exploration led to the questions of translation. How can factory-built modulars—no-frills boxes produced on an assembly line—be transformed into a traditional American bungalow? What are the nuances of interpretation that must be imposed? How do those distinctions of the Arts and Crafts style affect the bottom line? Is prefab construction the right choice for this project?

Prefab is an umbrella term that covers a variety of factory-built houses and includes mobile, modular, panelized, and pre-cut kit homes. Mobile homes (now referred to as manufactured homes) were originally meant to be just that: mobile. Hence, the "trailer park" reputation of tin-can housing that could be hitched to the back of a pick-up truck and moved to a new location. Mobile homes are constructed entirely in a factory and then moved to a site location where they are placed on concrete slabs. Wheels are removed, and though they remain moveable, this rarely occurs. Panelized homes consist of factory-built walls (windows and doors included) that are shipped as one-dimensional units to be assembled on-site. Pre-cut

houses provide the elements in pre-sized and pre-shaped puzzle-type pieces to be put together by a builder using traditional means. Modular housing is factory-assembled in full-dimensional units. They are built to state and local building codes and must be installed on a foundation.

Modular construction was chosen for a variety of reasons. With industrial technology, quality control, product inspection every step of the way, and the building standards imposed by law, it seemed an unquestionably sound choice. Costs are controlled, as all materials are purchased in volume and technicians and craftsmen work as a team. Time, too, is economized, as construction continues in spite of weather, and the assembly line can run beyond the days and seasons for outdoor work.

Today's modular houses can range in size from 1,000 to 6,000 square feet and can be designed to accommodate everything from the simple needs and/or budgets of senior citizens or entry-level buyers, to the high-end designer style incorporated into this one. With average

MODULAR MINUTIAE: PRESENT

- More than 22 million Americans live in modular homes.
- 1995–2005 is known as "the Decade of Manufactured Housing" by the Manufactured Housing Industry.
- There are 275 manufactured-home facilities in America.
- About one in eight new single-family homes is modular.
- Manufactured housing retail sales totaled nearly $10 billion in 2002.
- Cost per square foot is 10 to 35 percent less than comparable site-built homes.
- Modular homes are factory-built to state codes and modules are transported to the site.

(Source: Manufactured Housing Institute at www.mfghome.org)

(**Opposite Page**) View of a modular being moved into place.

(**Left**) A modular is moved into place. (**Above Left**) A modular unit is lifted from a truck. (**Above Right**) The master bedroom wing is lifted from a flatbed delivery trailer, ready for placement beside the center unit's living areas.

costs ranging from 10 to 25 percent less than stick-built, modular homes offer an affordable choice. In the past this affordability provided housing (and commercial buildings) on a limited budget. With this house in the Berkshires, the designer translated the savings on construction costs into high-end features, elaborate details, beautiful furnishings, and unique accessories.

Many of the misconceptions surrounding modular housing are just that. Their reputation as cheap, boring, and of poor construction was perhaps earned during the 1970s and 1980s when builders lined developments with hastily assembled homes

that could be had for reasonable rates. The notion of modular homes as simply "double-wides"—boxes dropped on undeveloped suburban and rural spaces—may reflect on years of production of single-story, two-unit connections that lacked any distinguishing features. However, in the past decade, design improvements and technological innovations have moved modular construction into a whole new realm. High standards are maintained both at the factory level and through local agencies that impose strict code enforcement. The most important innovation of the past five years has been the development of two-story models. This step forward

has been made possible through factory expansion, engineering, materials improvement, and, perhaps most importantly, improved transportation potential.

Having settled on the use of modular construction, it was time to begin in earnest. The first step toward moving a home from imagination to realization is purchasing the property that will become the building site. For this project, a plot of land in the beautiful Berkshire Mountains of Massachusetts provided the rich surrounding landscape that was to be reflected in this new American bungalow. Of course, there is no substitute for natural beauty, but practical matters must first be put

(**Above**) A factory worker removes the wrap from the top of the module to prepare for attaching a crane and cables for lifting and setting. (**Right**) The second-floor bedroom is lifted from a flatbed delivery truck and moved toward placement.

to rest. Can the appropriate building certificates be obtained? How does the cost of land affect the overall budget? What are the expenses associated with land clearing and site preparation? What are the local zoning and building requirements? Surely there is no fonder hope than nestling a country cottage amid the trees and native foliage; but first the practical realities must be dealt with. Most of the questions concerning land use and permit requirements can be answered with a call to the local building and zoning offices; here again, the modular company can help provide assistance and direction.

The property chosen for this project was more expensive than originally budgeted for; but crunching the numbers showed that the savings on the house itself allowed for what may have been beyond affordability. The real estate mantra "location, location, location" seemed confirmation enough for an investment in this property; its proximity to New York and Boston added value to this pristine woodland. In addi-

tion, the site had been cleared earlier, and many approvals were already in place. Since the property was located in a new development area, it was also important at this point to be sure that delivery of the modules would be possible. Trucks carrying seven 15-ton boxes had to be accommodated; 4,500 square feet of real estate had to be transported into the woods. Luckily, this was one of the many details that the modular company handled.

And how can we choose a modular company that is, indeed, accommodating? Time for some legwork: research, investigate, visit the factory, and ask for all of the information you will need to make your decision. Look for good response time to your phone

calls. If calls go unreturned for more than forty-eight hours, make the company or dealer aware of your frustrations, and if slow response continues, look elsewhere. If they drag their feet in getting information to you, it often means that the project is not significant to them and you'll get lost in the shuffle. Once pricing details have been supplied to you, ask about the "fudge factor." Beware of open-ended estimates that would significantly alter the bottom line. If there are a number of questionable or outstanding figures because the company is not sure of pricing, pin down the amounts or walk away. For this project, the first choice of companies had to be rejected

(**Left**) A view from the outside into the basement area shows that another modular unit will soon be installed. (**Right**) Unfinished basement interior shows framing and Lally columns that have been installed to offer support of modules on the main floor.

(Left) A tractor transports a finished unit from the factory to the outside storage/loading area. (Above Left) Designer Michael Buchanan and Simplex Marketing Director Dave Boniello go over final details before delivery day opens. (Above Right) Views of the outside storage/loading area where completed units are prepared for delivery and await loading onto flatbed trucks.

six months after talks had begun and the redesigning process was nearly complete. In spite of Better Business Bureau approval and good references from former customers, the company failed to fit the needs of our project goals. A new company was sought out, and the replacement turned out to be better than the original.

Simplex Industries, located in Scranton, Pennsylvania, may have hedged at first; but it was not long before they recognized how the value of design influences would eventually bring growth and profit to their business. They jumped on board with a team of experts who not only understood the project but were also respectful of the

expertise brought to it by the architect and designer. From the president on down to the receptionist, there was a level of curiosity and professionalism that never wavered throughout the course of their involvement.

The lesson is that whether a house is stick-built or factory-built, construction brings with it frustrations and difficulties that can only be resolved in an atmosphere of mutual trust and understanding. If you do not choose carefully from the beginning, you may find that advantages never will outweigh disadvantages if you are working with a manufactured-housing company that is simply committed to producing

cookie-cutter, box-like structures. In some ways, buying a modular home is not unlike buying a car. Factories that produce them have distributors who sell them and local builders who construct them; many dealers have model homes—showcase examples that consumers can walk through to get a better feel. Auto dealers can let you take a car for a test drive—but even though you can't eat or sleep in a modular model, you can get a sense of its features, dimensions, layout, and material use. Then you can customize through the dealer. In many cases you can even arrange for a tour of the factory to watch the assembly process.

You will also find that many of the modular homes are sold factory-direct—as was the case with Simplex. The Internet is an invaluable tool in finding modular companies—a simple search can turn up many outlets and pages of information.

The next lesson centered on the architectural process. The project architect, Timothy Langan, produced drawings to the sizes and dimensions that were appropriate for the modular components. It was thought that by doing so a big step in time and decision-making would be taken. Unfortunately this was not the case. The modular company had to take

(**Above**) Inside the factory storage area: lumber purchased in bulk reduces building costs. It is also kept out of the weather for use as needed in production. (**Opposite Page**) Work on a modular unit begins with flooring. Here a worker attaches decking to floor joists.

the drawings and translate them into their own format and vocabulary. This would enable them to get signed and sealed drawings from the state to which the home was being delivered. The amount of time it took to re-create the drawings was approximately two weeks—surprisingly fast, actually—but time was becoming critical due to outside pressures to complete the house.

Most modular companies offer a variety of home styles to choose from, with floor plans, standard construction specifications, and option packages included in their brochures. Computers are used to generate and incorporate design changes, and many companies offer architectural services. Choosing a standard model, of course, requires no additional input from an architect. However, for this project, the designer's determination to make extraordinary changes in such elements as the roofline and to add bungalow-style details made collaboration with an architect necessary. In addition, when the project first got under way,

no modular company had yet been chosen.

A FACTORY TOUR

A visit to the Simplex Industries modular factory was an eye-opening and amazing experience. Generally speaking, a factory-built house is on the assembly line for five days; the Simplex assembly time per house is two-and-one-half days from start to finish. Knowing that the house was being constructed in half the time seemed impossible and raised concerns that the quality would be inferior. However, the end results offered a pleasant surprise to the contrary: the speed and efficiency of the factory, as well as the level of finish and quality of installation, were all top-notch.

Unlike site-built homes, which begin with exterior framing and roofing, modular homes are built from the inside out. Not only are high-quality materials used to assemble the framework, but wallboard is both screwed and glued to the stud walls. Because of the need to protect against damage in delivery, additional

steel plates are used to maintain rigidity, and 20 to 30 percent more lumber is used in the framing. Industry spokesmen often point out that the extra durability needed for travel means factory-built is sturdier than site-built.

Assembly begins with the flooring, and factory engineers insure that the layout and strength will provide adequate support to the rest of the structure: 2 x 10 floor joists are an industry standard, and most offer floor decking that is 3/4-inch tongue-and-groove plywood. Front and rear perimeters are double 2 x 10 framing, and each module includes double 2 x 10s, with two laminate

(**Above**) The factory exterior. (**Right**) Inside the factory storage area.

(**Left**) A factory worker builds stairs.
(**Right**) Stacks and boxes of wood flooring.

areas at the mating, or marriage, walls (where units will be joined on-site). Wall panels are added next, and this includes R-19 insulation, electric and plumbing connections, and 1/2-inch drywall that is smooth-finished and prime-painted. The ceilings are smooth-finished as well and generally are insulated in the range of R-30 to R-38.

The installation of windows, doors, bath and kitchen fixtures, carpeting, and heating units begins once the framing and insulation are complete. Homeowners are given the option of custom finish for many of these items—whether they choose them as part of a package deal or simply opt for shopping on their own and shipping to the modular company for installation. Copper water supply

lines are used for plumbing, and there are such factory-installed features as shut-off valves for each toilet and sink and anti-scald shower valves. Baseboard electric heat with individual wall-mounted thermostats is commonly used, but other options such as natural gas and propane heating units can be accommodated.

The Manufactured Housing Institute states on their Web site (www.mfghome.org) that there are about 275 manufactured-home facilities in the United States today. Each may provide a choice of model homes and materials to be used, and each is

required by law to construct housing that meets with state and local building regulations. As such, there is a wide range of materials available for both interior and exterior use. Homeowners are free to choose their own materials, as well.

That said, there are some materials that are relied upon industry-wide for their proven quality, and these include sealed roof underlay, twenty-five-year roof shingles installed over felt paper, steel-insulated doors, and double-hung vinyl windows, siding, soffits, and fascia. Other exterior siding finishes are available, including wood

(**Above Left**) Workers secure wrapping so there is no damage during delivery. (**Right**) The crane moves into place for setting the first section of the second floor. This piece contains dormers, the gable roof end, and a second-floor doorway that will lead to a balcony.

and stucco, but these will add to the cost. Again, material use is determined by model chosen, the consumer's needs and budget, and by individual manufacturing companies. For this home, choosing materials was part of the process of customizing the home; information on those choices are detailed in later chapters.

Because this project was not standard, an extra day or two was required for the level of finish desired. Even watching the efficiency, it was hard to imagine that with only an extra day or two complicated millwork would be installed. This process in the field would take numerous days, if not weeks.

LIMITATIONS ON DESIGN

Even with all the pros of the modular method of construction, there are certain limitations that cannot be avoided. Our attempts to push the envelope were met with little success on several items— in spite of the willingness of Simplex to always accommodate expectations and demands. Certain building codes, pitch of roof, and structural engineering requirements dictated significant design details. The architect and engineer went back and forth on a typical roofline; unfortunately the engineer prevailed over the design team.

A long, sloping roof that could accommodate an overhang and allow for a continuous roofline to include a covered porch was the originally anticipated design. The factory was unable to construct the length and slope of the roof, and even if it could have been fabricated, the size would have been impossible to ship. This became a huge design dilemma because one key ingredient of the bungalow style is a severely sloping roof that incorporates a front porch.

One option that was suggested but not acted on was to have the contractor build the roof on-site. This idea seemed to defeat the purpose of the economy of time, materials, and money in using modular construction. The end result was to modify the drawings to maintain a certain roof slope but not to include a roof that would extend to a covered porch. Creating a porch in a bungalow style with an arbor was finally settled on as a good design solution.

Other design alterations had to be made due to building codes, wind velocity, shipping, and factory capabilities. The additional changes were

(**Above Left**) In the dining room, crown molding is from Style Solutions; an inexpensive directional light fixture was purchased from a local home retailer. (**Above Right**) A glass doorknob on an interior door (reproduction hardware from Emtek) adds a touch of old-world elegance. (**Right**) Tile installation in the master bathroom will be completed before delivery.

not as difficult as the impact of changing the roof design. In the end it seemed that each time the design had to be reworked, it got even better. And while each of these design changes brought with it an additional cost, the budget was able to withstand the added costs due to the savings gained through the use of modular construction.

Obviously, the cost for any home is dependent upon size, location, and the number of amenities included. Generally speaking, it is estimated that modular homes are 10 to 25 percent cheaper than stick-built. The only way to make a specific cost comparison is to do your homework: what is the average cost per square foot for stick construction and how does that compare to the cost per square foot for modular?

Financing for modular homes is available through local lending agencies and banks, and options include financing for land and home together. Modular dealers often can arrange for financing and direct you toward local lending agencies, or you can

(Left) A worker cuts and trims hardwood flooring along corners and doorjambs. (Right) Tools and wood flooring.

proceed independently. Terms are similar to traditional home mortgage financing, with thirty-year terms and secondary market sources (such as Fannie Mae) available.

CHAPTER 3

" EVEN THOUGH THE WHOLE PROJECT
HAD COME TOGETHER SO EASILY, BOTH IN THE FACTORY AND ON-SITE,
THERE WAS STILL MUCH WORK TO BE DONE, ESPECIALLY BECAUSE OF
THE DESIGNER DETAILS AND INTRICATE FINISHING DESIRED. "

DESIGN RECIPE FOR A MODULAR BUNGALOW

The final details of wood flooring are completed at the factory just before the unit is ready for delivery.

The goal for this project was to build a prefab twenty-first-century bungalow: to create a house that looked like it had evolved over time. The structure was meant to have the appearance of a rambling country farmhouse whose wings were added a generation after the main house was built. The objective was to depict a natural progression. Here would be a new modular house, nestled in the mountains and looking like it had been there through the years.

Once the initial site preparation had been completed and the units had been assembled at the factory, the time for delivery approached. In this early stage of laying the groundwork, another example of how modular construction can save time emerged: while the outside land was made ready for the foundation, the construction process continued at the factory. In addition to the excavation needed to carve a level area into the land for the foundation, this phase includes septic preparation and installation, rough plumbing to provide for waste fittings, and placement of primary underground electrical service.

All modular housing must be placed on a foundation; homeowners may choose traditional poured concrete or a pre-cast paneling system

that means saving time and money. The foundation for this project was manufactured and installed by Superior Walls of America. The panels are assembled horizontally at the factory and are made of an outside wall of high-strength concrete combined with reinforced concrete pillars. Styrofoam insulation gives the walls an R-5 rating (as opposed to the R-2 factor of concrete blocks) and pressure-treated furring strips are attached to each pillar to accommodate drywall finishing. Panels are joined using pre-installed saddle bolts, and polyurethane caulking with concrete adhesives insures a tight seal between panels. With no

waiting for materials to set, complete installation can be accomplished in less than a day.

With the foundation in place, it was time for delivery. Seven 15-ton modules with 15-plus-foot-wide sections were shrink-wrapped and loaded on flatbed trucks. Leaving as the sun rose, they made their way north: 225 miles through the interstates of Pennsylvania, along the New York State Thruway, and finally proceeding along a ten-mile stretch of rural Massachusetts roads. Prior to delivery, Simplex did the highway-transport paperwork—securing various state permits and scouting the route for any

(Far Left) A crewman stands in the basement foundation area as a cameraman shoots a partially finished modular set.
(Above Right) Delivery trucks from Simplex Industries have completed the nearly 225-mile trek to the home site. The final leg of that journey is along this narrow country road.
(Right) The set crew views the center unit placement on the foundation.

(**Opposite Page**) Living room set in place; temporary support members will be removed once the set is complete, and finish work will begin.
(**Above**) Kitchen modular unit set in place: note that the cabinets have been tied securely for the delivery. (**Left**) Electrical finish work will not require any cut-ins once on-site—they are completed at the factory for easier connections once the home is ready to be wired.

(Left) Midpoint break: workers rest surrounded by the empty flatbeds as the halfway point is reached. First- and second-floor modules are now securely in place. (Above Left) A set crewman takes a look at the module before it is removed from a delivery truck. (Above Right) Loading/storage lot: all units are ready for their journey to Massachusetts.

potential problems. Once the trucks arrive, an 80-ton crane becomes the workhorse. Crews secure heavy-duty cables to pick-up points on each section so a uniform weight distribution is maintained and there is no chance for bowing or bending of the framework.

A heavy-duty crane is used to install the units atop the foundation. Skilled workmen, known as the set crew, insure proper alignment with adjoining modules. Using a tool known in the industry as a "come-along," workmen join adjacent units into a marriage, or mating, point, where factory preparations will allow for on-site finish work to secure the

units. Until all walls are joined, Lally columns are installed in the basement to support the first-floor beams. The steel brackets that connect the units at the marriage wall have been designed so the finish work on-site consists primarily of bolting the pieces together and then removing any supports that were added for shipping.

In just two days, this extraordinary creation had been delivered and assembled. The first floor, which contains the living room, dining room, sunroom, laundry/utility room, and bath, is composed of two units. Two more modules were used to create

Design Recipe for a Modular Bungalow   77

(**Above and Lower Right**) The sunroom module is wrapped and ready for shipment. (**Opposite Page**) The dining room niche as it hovers midair and a crane operator moves it into place.

the second floor and its two bed-rooms and baths, and another unit became the spacious master bed-room wing. The final two were indeed icing on the cake: the dramatic roof pieces that had been designed to cre-ate the bungalow style. Triangular end pieces form the peak of the gable roof and the two hinged sides (which have been folded for shipping) are joined together. The 4,500-square-foot home stood proud and secure, ready for its final on-site finishing. Even though the whole project had come together so easily, both in the

factory and on-site, there was still much work to be done, especially because of the designer details and intricate finishing desired.

Approaching the tasks for the finishing phase requires more home-work, planning, and decision-making. Most modular companies can provide direction and recommendations but essentially their work is done. Unless you have purchased the home from a modular builder who specializes only in modular finish work, you will have to arrange for various trade and craftsmen to complete the work. You

(**Left**) The rear exterior view shows that four modular units have been set in place.
(**Right**) Factory work on the master bathroom: Kohler vanities are installed.

(**Left**) Workers install kitchen utilities; sink and plumbing are all placed before delivery. (**Right**) Designer/owner Michael Buchanan makes final notes on house plans.

may choose to hire a general contractor to oversee and coordinate the subcontractors who will provide the final services. Whatever direction you opt for, it is important to secure and confirm these estimates with the modular company. They are familiar with the range of pricing for such things as electrical and plumbing tie-ins, and they may be able to offer solutions when prices seem out of range. Of course, there is plenty of finish work that can be completed by the homeowner; with walls and woodwork pre-primed, painting can easily be done by do-it-yourselfers. Perhaps the most important thing to remember at this stage is that progress slows considerably, and it's hard to be prepared for such slow-downs when the building itself has been constructed so quickly.

The finish work for this project started with the exterior siding and roofing. In order to achieve the designer's vision of a house that had grown and changed over time, various building materials were incorporated for the exterior and interior details: a galvanized roof on the main house, simulated cedar shakes on the wings, board-and-batten siding on the master bedroom wing, and clapboard and shake on the main body. Each of these choices reflected the goal not only of creating a dynamic house but also of using the important hallmarks of the Arts and Crafts aesthetic.

If there is one single defining element that is basic to the bungalow exterior, it is the exaggerated rooflines. Adding this important emphasis required that the master bedroom wing details be integrated

Design Recipe for a Modular Bungalow   83

(**Opposite Page**) A view of the stairway from the entrance foyer to the second-floor landing. Stairs have been installed at the factory and will be finished on-site. (**Left**) Close-up of unfinished entry foyer; the storage/bench seating area tucked under the stairway area is an interesting detail added by the designer and installed at the factory. (**Below**) View of dining room bump-out with framing that has been installed for delivery. The frames will be removed during finishing, and this will become the dining room.

with the main house. By extending the overhang to 24 inches (versus the typical 6–10 inches), a harmonious effect was achieved. Arts and Crafts bracket details on the gable ends give the appearance that they are structurally necessary to support the elongated overhang. But they are only decorative—relatively inexpensive accents that confirm the bungalow style while personalizing the modular's austerity.

Another detail that integrates the wing addition to the whole is the combination of sidings. There are cedar shakes on both the main house

and on the gable end of the wing; however, a switch from clapboard to board and batten was implemented for the wing siding. Since bungalows were known for their interesting mix of building materials and for seeking economy whenever possible, this was a good alternative. Because it is less expensive to buy and install, board-and-batten siding is often thought of as cheap—and, not unlike modular housing, it may have gained this reputation a decade or so ago. During the building boom of the mid-1970s and the 1980s, excessive use of T-111 siding—a plywood siding with

(**Above Left**) Wrapping used for delivery is removed from the roof-section module as it is prepared for installation. (**Above Right**) Bracket details inset on roof overhangs show a great way to reiterate the Craftsman feel on the exterior without spending a fortune; these were purchased off the rack. (**Opposite Page**) The exterior front elevation awaits the installation of columns on stone piers, crowned off with an open-rafter cedar pergola with decorative end tails.

(Left) Close-up of a pier with faux stone veneer; wooden columns will be built atop the piers and then used to support the exterior pergola to add a bungalow feel to the front entrance.
(Right) Owens Corning Cultured Stone is a man-made stone product that is molded from natural stones; however, pumice used as filler with Portland cement creates a much lighter product.

grooves to simulate board and battens—was heavily used. There is a fear that when traditional board and batten is used it may be perceived as T-111 siding. Here it proved to be an excellent choice: the application not only looks sophisticated and refined but also makes the wing appear to have perhaps been a carriage house that was added to the main structure.

The use of stone was a way that Arts and Crafts architects hoped to achieve the appearance of a house that was a natural extension of the land. Stone cladding was added to the foundation here and was also used as another central but simple ingredient in the designer's recipe: bungalow columns. Not unlike the catalog/kit houses of a century ago, the columns (purchased "off the rack" from a catalog/Internet company) would become an important architectural element. Solidly built wooden pedestals that broadened at the base were added to both the front and rear of the dwelling. Supported by stone-clad piers, they add texture and interest.

Large multipaned windows with transoms are used throughout; both window and door grilles are simple and more evocative of the Prairie style than the shingle style of traditional French door grilles. Natural cedar siding and trim are used throughout, and rich colors on eligible clapboard enhance the beauty of the exposed natural shakes.

Since an Arts and Crafts–style roofline could not be achieved in modular construction, a search through Aladdin, Benedict, and Sears house catalogs led to the design of an open pergola that would add another

architectural element and provide support for beautiful flowering vines. The greenery would be a subtle counterpoint in harmony with the natural landscape, and the structure itself would add emphasis to the Arts and Crafts style.

The inspiration for another detail for the arbor came quite unexpectedly during a visit to the nearby Edith Wharton home, The Mount. A master decorator whose seminal work on the decoration of houses influences much of the interior design of this house, Wharton created magnificent gardens to surround her estate. A walk through the garden with the project architect turned our eyes to the extraordinary detail she incorporated into the arbors. These interesting end tails were sketched and then enlarged for the carpenters to use as templates in their creation. The cedar arbor, supported by stone piers and flared columns, were now embellished with a touch of Wharton.

Landscaping is the crowning glory of the exterior—unexpectedly simple, perhaps, but once again reminiscent of kinship with the Arts and Crafts movement. Not unlike Frank Lloyd Wright's integration of house

(Left) Exterior rear view as seen through the surrounding trees on a winter day.
(Right) Stone-clad piers show a typical Arts and Crafts detail; stone veneer product made it easy and inexpensive to use.

(**Left**) A beautiful spring day allows for a festive gathering on the spacious deck just outside the kitchen.

(**Right**) The completed front porch is a great place for Pete to run (and his owners to rest).

and landscape, here is an uncontrived and minimal approach. In early spring and summer, a proliferation of mosses and ferns forms a carpet for a row of birch trees that bring a splash of white to otherwise deep forest green. There are protruding rocks and remnants of an old stone wall that give depth to the surrounds and to the setting of the house sheltered in the woodlands.

CHAPTER 4

"THE BEST OF AMERICAN DESIGN INTEGRATES
A VARIETY OF STYLES; AND IT'S ALL DONE WITH A KEEN
EYE FOR SCALING PROPORTIONS AND
MAINTAINING SENSITIVITY TO TEXTURE AND TONE."

(**Left**) An eclectic guest bedroom filled with a variety of styles and periods of antiques.

f the blending of styles and materials on the exterior of the house sounds like a hodgepodge, it could be; however, with a designer's eye, the mixture can create a home loaded with character and charm. As various elements are combined to reflect a wider sense of time and place, the overall design must still maintain a sense of balance and proportion to create harmony—and this merging of styles, periods, colors, and textures holds true for both the exterior design and interior decorating. Just as the very structure of the house was meant to appear to be rooted in the past but not forgotten by our time, so, too, was the interior meant to reflect and evoke such a feel.

The approach to this interior could be equally seen as a hodgepodge, as the designer's goal was to create an old-world flavor that recalled our mosaic heritage and reflected our cherished traditions of home. Capturing the essence of a time and place gone by was important—as was avoiding the creation of a period Arts and Crafts or bungalow museum room. Instead it was hoped to evoke a prewar feeling and not to re-create what people would expect the interior

to look like because of the exterior bungalow details.

Good design principles apply to every interior, regardless of architecture, design, or construction style. Distinctive décor is often non-conformist, encompassing a variety of styles. Balance is everything: refined color classics next to whimsical primitives lend the most wonderful flavor of comfort and personality. The best of twenty-first-century American design integrates a variety of styles; and it's all done with a keen eye for scaling proportions and maintaining sensitivity to texture and tone. A contradiction in styles and periods can be

transformed into a grand and sophisticated statement.

Architect Charles Moore once defined his craft this way: "Architecture is the choreography of the familiar and the surprising." A successful designer also embraces the notion of the unexpected—creating interiors that are at once demure and seductive, understated and bold. You won't find the expected brick fireplace or a small cluster of rooms in this house. This house has breathing room and the ambience of graceful aging. The sparse "too new" feeling that often marks new construction has been mitigated with antique furnishings, rich patterns and colors, and the effect of layers and lighting.

In addition to applying good design principles, for most of us it is equally important to keep an eye on the bottom line. And while establishing a budget may seem an easy enough task, sticking to the numbers may not be so easy. The interiors described here were accomplished on-budget by applying a "good, better, best" philosophy. Simply stated, this

(**Left**) English printed wallpaper adorns the walls of the first-floor powder room and a mosaic tabletop forms a floor medallion that is coordinated with the beautiful Kohler bronze fixtures. (**Right**) The seating/reading nook on the second-floor landing is another example of eclecticism; the combination of fabrics was meant to convey the feeling of treasures found on whirlwind travels.

philosophy's mantra is "save wherever you can and then splurge with the savings." Examples of how this works can be seen throughout this project.

ENTRY FOYER

If a home's exterior can be likened to the cover on a book, then the entry foyer is perhaps comparable to that moment of opening a fascinating book that beckons you to continue. As a space whose function is for circulation, transition, and setting the tone, the foyer's importance cannot be denied.

The decorating scheme here is bolder and more dramatic than initially planned. Realtors may espouse the belief that bright and cheery are the easiest sells; shelter magazines may love the look of an open beach-house feel; but neither really captured the feeling of drama that was needed here. And what has more drama than rich, saturated red? The color was chosen in spite of the decorating challenges it created and in spite of the contractor's opinion that it would never work in such an open foyer. It was a moment all designers and do-it-yourselfers have faced—but sometimes decisions that seem outlandish at first, work out beautifully in the end.

The color sets off the staircase magnificently. Instead of the balustrades just blending in, their graceful, twisted silhouettes are accentuated by the bold color. Two black Empire side chairs make a grand statement, as does the 1940s mahogany console table with beautiful lines and bad veneer problems. This $100 find was painted a matte black; and while some may balk at painting wood, paint not only hides a myriad of sins but can also be the common element that ties disjointed elements together.

The all-important entrance lighting was found at a home center: blackened bronze sconces with a choice of shades provide ambience and charm for about $25, as do the halogen surface-mounted lights purchased at the same home center for even less. The savings here went toward another splurge: an unfinished painting by an artist whose works imitate Norman Rockwell's

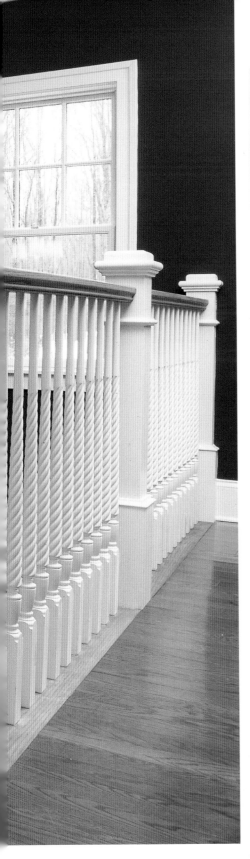

(**Left**) The entrance foyer features a newel post with modern finial and a mixture of antique styles to complement the rich red walls and white trim. (**Opposite Page and Below**) Two views of the second-floor landing; one is of a Victorian Gothic chair juxtaposed with a modern art–style painting hung above to emphasize the eclecticism of the Arts and Crafts movement.

Saturday Evening Post covers that was purchased for about $600. The runner is also a top-quality item that ties in all the colors beautifully. An inexpensive Louis XVI chair with existing upholstery (a great find at $85) was added; even though the color is a little more pink than red, all the white in the plaid makes it a good fit and a strong graphic statement.

KITCHEN AND DINING ROOM

Beyond this visually striking entry are the kitchen and dining room. Each was designed to feel like a step into another time and place, as twenty-first-century updates and amenities have been discreetly tucked away. Central air-conditioning, a sound system, ample storage, a six-burner gas and electric stove, and state-of-the-art appliances outfit the kitchen. And yet the eyes are drawn to the soft echoes of a much older kitchen; for the decoration and finish are sympathetic to period bungalow style. Natural cherry cabinets are rescued from the mundane with hand-finished hardware, decorative metal details, and glass-front doors with Prairie-style mullions. Natural marble tiles and hand-blocked wallpaper in the Willow Bough pattern from the William Morris period collection add color and warmth. Decorative objects and the vintage artwork continue the transport of this kitchen to an earlier time. Lighting is especially important in a kitchen, and a good plan incorporates a full spectrum of elements that

(Left) Guest room detail of antique European chest and accessories.
(Right) Dining room corner vignette featuring Sanderson & Sons, Ltd., period Arts and Crafts wallpaper with a combination of new and antique furnishings and accessories.

(**Left**) A state-of-the-art kitchen is outfitted with Merillat cherry cabinets with hand-hammered iron hardware; Zodiac solid-surface countertops from Corian; period reproduction William Morris Willow Bough wallpaper from England's Sanderson & Sons; and all of the latest appliances. (**Right**) Carved brackets added to built-in dining room cabinetry; this photo shows three fiberglass brackets installed under upper cabinets. Purchased for $10 each and then painted, they provide a designer detail and add sophistication.

are combined for task, function, sparkle, and ambience. Here halogen fixtures are used around the perimeter; these are combined with a center ceiling fan with multifunction light and indirect under-cabinet lights that provide subtle accents.

The dining room and kitchen flow into each other, but the dining room is actually a separate room with a casual and comfortable approach. For many homeowners, the dining room/area is often a space that becomes difficult to define. What is its function in today's lifestyle? Should it be formal or informal? What's practical about a room that is used for holidays only? How can this

much valuable space be both special and ordinary?

Here a small intimate table (that can be expanded to seat ten to twelve) suggests a dining space that can be used on an everyday basis, but beyond the table is a bump-out that creates a cozy seating niche. This area reflects an architectural detail that would have been common in a period home. High-quality custom upholstery is English linen floral from London's Sanderson & Sons, Ltd., and plush goose-down cushions sit atop hand-tiled, hard-rock maple frames from Avery Boardman, Ltd. (This affordable custom upholstery house is well known for its comfortable sleep sofas with mattress and box spring.) In front of the sofa is a hand-painted, heavily worn cocktail table picked up for just over $100. It's all pulled together with a wool sisal carpet with leather border—a freebie from the used-furniture store where the bedroom set was purchased.

The walls are covered in another period William Morris wallpaper (also from Sanderson & Sons) in soft greens and cream. Bungalows would typically have built-ins, and nestled in the corner are the same cabinets that were used in the kitchen. The natural cherry base and top cabinets with glass doors and mullions painted cream give it a custom look, as do the handsome resin brackets purchased off the rack for $10. A hand-carved, painted, and gilded Scandinavian chandelier that breaks away from a heavy-handed bungalow design is added to hand-finished hardware and handmade decorative items to complete the warm and inviting look. The palette of soft green, light cream, and cherry brown brings the outdoors in; the visual pleasure of the natural woodland setting is in perfect harmony with the shelter that rests in its splendor.

LIVING ROOM

The grand and elegant proportions of this room (at 18 feet 9 inches x 39 feet 9 inches, it is the size of three rooms) and the desire to make it the home's centerpiece made it the perfect place to rely on the designer's "good, better, best" school of decorating. Light blue on the ceiling and a rich warm cream on the walls provide take-your-breath-away color, especially set against the framing of cream acanthus-leaf crown molding. But it is the spectacular fireplace mantel that commands your attention. As the most prominent element of the room, it provides a focal point and defines everything else. It is not the price tag that establishes its importance but rather the scale and proportion along with finish. This hand-carved European limestone mantel would have used up a huge amount of the room's budget. The solution was to buy the floor

The living room corner vignette shows an interesting display of accessories, most of which were purchased at local thrift stores.

Typically, Arts and Crafts–style rooms would have a darker coloring and appearance, mainly due to the use of unpainted, natural wood trim. But twenty-first-century design is more about creating light, airy spaces with uncluttered decors. The living room not only captures that contemporary feeling but also evokes an earlier era with its grand architectural details.

model; a few minor dings meant saving thousands of dollars. The surround is considered the "best" in the room because of its location and size, and no expense was spared in showcasing it.

A majority of the upholstered furnishings for the room were chosen from what the designer calls the "better" category, and many of the items were purchased as seen without any reupholstery done. (Reupholstering is wonderful, but if frugality requires you to make it work "as is," you can often work with this challenge to create a cohesive statement.)

The elements that would be considered a part of the "good" category would be the rag-rolled rug (about $150 for a 9 x 12) that turned out to be the perfect choice because of its great colors and wonderful texture. Usually the rug should be of high quality, but in this instance with the focus being on the mantel, the rug did not inspire the decorating. Scattered throughout the room are Wedgwood accessories that would be considered the best; and while not all

of the accessories are top-notch, the visually important ones are. Such accessories can be seen on the cocktail table, the skirted round table next to the sofa, and sprinkled on a tall hutch that has open shelving.

The elegance of another era that perhaps may call for this room to be a "company only" parlor has been softened with all of the comforts of today's living. There is a classic formality here, and like a formal garden, tranquility is found in the careful order and form.

SUNROOM

The sunroom is the only room with a vaulted ceiling. A panelized roofing system allows for a full cathedral ceiling, and along with the visually expansive ceiling height, the room is outfitted with large windows on three sides. Warm antique yellow pine floors and a consistent color scheme of khaki, shades of rose, and muted green walls complete the look. Natural linen floral fabrics adorn the custom-made upholstery produced by Calico Corners, a retail establishment that is an excellent resource for either off-the-rack items or a customized designer order. The Calico Corners design experts are helpful with decorating dilemmas, and their good-quality merchandise can be seen here in the sunroom and in the upstairs bedroom. The furnishings in each are handmade, with felt interlining that gives a sumptuous, ball-gown appearance. The bargain of the room is the English tray-top cocktail table with aged bronze top and bamboo legs purchased at an antiques store for $65. A hand-knotted plush rug anchors the furniture and ties the colors together. Beyond that, it is the light that calls you into this room to be nourished and inspired.

(**Left**) Detail of corner of the rose-and-linen sofa located in the sunroom; note the designer details on this retail furniture from Calico Corners, including aged bronze nail heads and contrasting cording. (**Right**) The sunroom has designer furnishing purchased through a Calico Corners retail store; all are made with luxurious fabrics and sumptuous trimmings, with draperies of rich textures and colors.

(**Left**) Sunroom décor shows how layering of decorative details adds visual height to relate the ceiling to a more human scale and draw the eye to take it all in. Note the Prairie-style doors that lead to the living room. (**Right**) The hallway to the master bedroom wing shows off-the-rack cabinets that have been built in to provide storage as well as a small bench/window seat. The built-ins were prominent in bungalow-style homes and are practical and architecturally more interesting than just a walled hallway.

MASTER BEDROOM AND BATH

The master bedroom and bath feature typical modular framing; but architectural elements have been added: the "tented" ceiling in each room is surrounded by intricately carved 13-inch crown molding, and 10-inch baseboard provides a richly finished border.

The master bath has a wall treatment of Arts and Crafts wainscot paneling clad on four walls, creating a color scheme that is more Parisian than English. French limestone flooring surrounds a stately cast-iron soaking tub centered on an exterior wall and a tiled shower centered on the opposite. The tub is flanked by two mahogany vanities with inset porcelain sinks. All of the master bath fixtures and fittings (as well as others throughout the house) are part of the Kohler product line. They feature both a contemporary and traditional line; traditional elements were chosen for use here.

A variety of light sources illuminate the cavernous space, and a fantastic antique rock crystal chandelier crowns the room. The chandelier is often referred to as the jewelry of the room, and if a label were to be attached to this one, it would be Cartier—as it is an extremely high-quality and

(**Left**) The master bedroom is outfitted with sumptuous silk and cotton fabrics purchased from a local thrift store. Original design could command a cost as high as $14,000; the seven pieces used here (including a hand-tied mattress) were purchased for $1,200. (**Opposite Page Top**) A dresser in the master bedroom and wall decoration show how the designer uses stacking of an art collection and accessories to create a rich and stylish look. (**Opposite Page Bottom**) The master bedroom seating area has a cozy corner with a large over-stuffed club chair with multicolored fabrics and trimmings.

(**Left**) Guest room vignette of an eighteenth-century Italian screen with primitive garden accessories brought indoors. (**Right**) The master bath shower area in a room that was meant to look like a period room that had been retrofitted to become a bath features French limestone floors from Ann Sacks. The modular company installed the Arts and Crafts wall paneling and Style Solutions neo-classical crown molding was added on-site. An antique English chair and copper garden finial complete the look of a garden-room bath that opens to a balcony.

eye-opening piece (see page 140). The goal for this room was to create the appearance of a room that had already existed and had been retrofitted into a bathroom. The sconces flanking the medicine cabinets are "good"—purchased from a local home center for about $30, while the four halogens were also purchased from a home center for $12 each. They do not look inexpensive, however, and provide another example of the good, better, best equation.

The color palette for the master bedroom is lighter, with many accents in shades of red and green. All too often this red/green color combination comes with the pitfall of creating a Christmas flavor; but rich, deep tones can save you from that concern. Here the shades are soft and muted, with splashes of the bolder tones. The floors are reconstituted 100-year-old yellow pine with wonderful aged luster throughout. The furniture was purchased at a second-hand store—and here was the deal of the century: seven pieces plus a custom-made high-end mattress for $1,200. The set with mattress included

Updating Arts and Crafts Detail   119

could easily sell for $15,000. The bedding is a splurge: a custom bed spread with silk taffeta bed skirt that looks like a million bucks and was worth every dime. The mattress mentioned is a custom handmade mattress and box spring, and while some may cringe at the thought of used bedding, remember that hotel bedding has always been used by someone else. A fortune was saved, and quality was not compromised; that's the goal for any frugal decorator.

UPSTAIRS GUEST BEDROOM AND BATH

European splendor could describe this gorgeous oasis. The room has all the charm of a prewar room in a Swedish country house, with soft romantic colors and elegant neo-classical antique furnishings. It also has a beautiful fireplace mantel that was purchased for $350 (vs. $3,800 for the one in the living room). The money saved on the mantel was used on custom draperies for the large window. A variety of good to better to best antiques furnish this room, all tied together with a handmade Aubusson rug of creams, blues, pinks, and greens.

The guest bathroom on the second floor proclaims the style of the 1930s with its marble mosaic tile border and field of herringbone white marble. Retro ceramic tiles clad the walls of the generously sized shower, and a retro, stainless steel-legged vanity with porcelain top suggests something salvaged from an antique house. The beautiful Sanderson & Sons lilac-patterned wallpaper not only brings the outdoors in but also adds a colorful softness to what could be a sterile room. A combination of antique lighting and new sconces blends beautifully in the room. The luxury of incorporating an exterior deck with plantings offers the planted English garden at your fingertips.

(**Left**) Draperies in the guest bedroom luxuriously lined for an elegant swathe. A hand-painted Italian breakfront is commanding in scale but not overwhelming. The French furniture and rug bring a European flair to the Berkshires.

(**Right**) A variety of styles are combined in the second-floor bedroom. Handmade silk drapery treatments complement the colors in the contemporary painting hanging above the Louis XVI caned-back chair.

CHAPTER 5

"THE SUCCESS OF A DECORATED ROOM IS THAT THE
VIEWER'S EYE INITIALLY WANDERS AROUND THE ROOM AND TAKES IT
ALL IN. THE EYE WILL STOP ON INDIVIDUAL ITEMS AFTER
IT HAS FEASTED ON THE BEAUTIFUL DÉCOR."

CREATING THE LOOK FOR LESS

Even with its light upholstery, the living room still appears to be comfortable and inviting—not that taboo space of our parents' or grandparents' generation. Silk pillows in purple and white checks add a whimsical note when paired with the antique patina of the furniture and accessories; they downplay the formal side of a newly constructed space with their charm.

During the design and construction of the Berkshire house, the modular factory expressed an interest in retaining the designer to create a model home on a more modest scale. They wanted as many bells and whistles and stylish details, but they also wanted the house to be affordable for entry-level buyers and middle-market clientele. Creating a knock-off version of the Berkshire high-style home was a goal that the designer was interested in pursuing; he was intrigued at the prospect of using what he had learned to produce the house for less. This unique opportunity for what essentially was to be a do-over is not one most consumers would have—but the valuable lessons can certainly be applied by paying attention to what this designer learned.

The most obvious way to cut the cost and create a look-for-less house was to reduce the size. In this case, the total square footage was cut nearly in half: from 4,500 square feet to 2,850 square feet. This may sound easy enough, given the computer technology that is used to generate plans, but changing room sizes and proportions as well as walkway space could not be done by simply having the computer reduce the plans in total by 20 to 25 percent. Instead the plans had to be reworked. This included flipping some rooms around, reducing circulation spaces, and then finally changing room sizes. Because the goal was to try to keep the airy, roomy feel throughout the house, cutting room dimensions was the place of last resort for cutting costs. Eventually the rooms did require some size reduction, but this turned out to be a minimal sacrifice to the overall house size, as previous cuts helped considerably.

The knock-off house was to be used as a model sales tool and a fresh new look at the modular company's capabilities. As such, it was constructed in proximity to the modular company grounds and site work was completed more efficiently. The house was also meant to be a source of inspiration for all price levels of modular housing. The goal was to inspire clients with designer details that could be added for little to no additional cost. These details could give a more customized look and add a client's own personal touch to their new home. For consumers, the house provides another tool for choosing options that can be included in whatever model is chosen.

Exterior details were altered, and this helped bring down the overall price of the house considerably. The roof overhang of the original house was reduced in size from 24 inches to 10 inches; vinyl eaves and siding were used instead of cedar. A less expensive window and door package, more affordable stone cladding, and finally an asphalt roof (versus the galvanized metal one) were added. The various cuts significantly altered the cost of the house; however, they did not lessen or cheapen the visual appearance. The biggest budget cut came from the change in column and front porch sizes. Creating a small porch turned out to be more successful than the expensive version; the columns appear larger and more visually commanding, and the pergola does not run across the entire front of the house. (The larger pergola impacts the interior lighting by lessening the light.) It is also an instance where

Entrance foyer as seen from the stairway; note how the crisp white balustrade details pop against the rich red walls.

(**Left**) Detail of living room mantel shows intricate carving and fine finish. The original antique version of this mantel would cost about $50,000, but Chesney's (a London-based company with showrooms in New York and Atlanta) replicated the limestone mantel in China with authentic hand-carved detail. This reproduction mantel was a bargain at $3,800, especially when compared with the cost of an original. (**Right**) Detail of concrete European-style mantel used in the second-floor guest bedroom. This simulated mantel, purchased for $350, was originally meant to be used in the living room. The designer felt that it lacked a commanding visual presence in that setting, but here it is a standout and an inviting focal point.

change can be beneficial both financially and visually.

Interior details were changed throughout. Some details were subtracted, others were added, and all were modified in some way. The overall visual appearance of the Massachusetts house has been substantially changed, but this Pennsylvania cousin still shines. A great deal of emphasis was placed on product sourcing so the look-for-less house would use more affordable items without compromising taste and style. One example was the budget for the fireplace mantel. The modular company's budget called for spending $300; the designer felt he needed $600. This may have at first seemed an impossible task, but with a lot of research and a designer's eye tweaking the delivered look, the mantels were purchased for $315 wholesale. They are a far cry from the $5,500 mantel used in the Berkshire home, but they are wonderful. There is no regret in using the more expensive one, because the positioning of the fireplace in that setting was more prominent than in the lower version house.

The high-end house had elaborate crown molding throughout; this one has the more expensive molding strategically placed in the public rooms to get the biggest bang for the buck. Wall paneling was still used throughout the house, but not as much as in the expensive one. The look-for-less house additions that had little bearing on the bottom line were a coffered ceiling in the dining room and a built-in window seat and bookshelf in the upstairs bedroom. These added architectural elements give instant character without affecting the bottom line.

A second bathroom was added upstairs in this house; this was done without impacting the budget because the fixtures used throughout the house were less expensive all

(**Left**) The bump-out section in the dining room creates a cozy niche. Surrounded by windows, this room is a light and comfortable place to gather before or after dinner. Here a green sofa with custom-made upholstery from Avery Boardman offers an inviting place to relax. The seating is clothed in a textural fabric collection from Sanderson & Sons, an English company known for their period florals and linens.
(**Right**) The guest bathroom with the sun streaming in on a winter day looks warm and inviting with its gorgeous floral wallpaper and white tile and trim.

around. Fiberglass showers and tub kits were used; sheet-vinyl flooring was used in two of the baths. In the master bath an inexpensive ceramic tile was placed on the diagonal, giving it a more expensive look. Only the master bath has the stone-top vanity; all the others have plastic laminate tops.

All of the bedrooms were carpeted,

versus hardwood floors with area rugs. Here area rugs were used on the carpets to visually break up the sea of carpet and to isolate different seating areas. By using carpeting instead of wood flooring, the savings were substantial. Another cost reduction was realized by painting the walls and using wallpaper borders to create a layered, finished look. The elegant

An antique English coffin carrier is transformed into a console table with the addition of an antique marble top to create a master bath vignette. The table is accessorized with vintage bath objects and a retro General Electric fan.

reproduction wallpaper used in the Berkshire home is so stunning that it would seem impossible to create such refinement without using it in the smaller home. But by carefully choosing the paint colors and wallpaper texture and design, the polished look was closely replicated.

The decorating for the second house was reduced greatly by using off-the-rack drapery treatments; in the dining room inexpensive shower curtains were used to create whimsical window treatments. Area rugs and almost all of the artwork and accessories were chosen from clearance aisles. There are no expensive lighting fixtures in the knock-off house, but you would not know by a passing glance. All of the fixtures are high-quality reproductions with antique hand finishes—high-end choices from a home center but still less expensive than antiques. Many accessories came from the Dollar Store, but you would have a hard time finding those items.

The success of a decorated room is that the viewer's eye initially wanders around the room and takes it all in first. Then after the initial wandering, the eye will stop on individual items after it has feasted on the beautiful décor. That was the goal of both houses, and judging from the viewers and comments, they are both successes. Whether you are an empty-nester looking to downsize or part of a growing family looking to up-size, modular construction can provide a design and price range to fit your needs. High-end, low-end, or something in between can become as unique and individual as your tastes demand and your budget requires. The sky's the limit!

DESIGN DIRECTIVES: DOS AND DON'TS

The more you know about the process of decorating, the better the end result will be. Creating surround-ings that are not only comfortable but also practical begins in the imag-ination, but giving shape and form to your dreams requires diligence and determination. There are many prac-tical and concrete ways to transform your vision into reality.

CREATE A SCRAPBOOK

Search through books and magazines and collect inspiration photos for each room. You may not find the exact room you are looking for, but a window treatment ad or table in a fin-ished room may be a part of what you envision. Don't be afraid to paste up your scrapbook with any elements you are drawn to, especially if you are unable to find a whole room you'd like to replicate. Think of your scrapbook as a book of scraps—bits and pieces from here and there that you will incorporate into the final design. Even as you gather inspiration from design publications, remember to choose styles that express your own personal style and identity. Remember that inspiration can come from nature, travel, catalogs, and decorator showcase rooms.

WRITE A DESCRIPTION OF YOUR DREAM ROOM

Begin with the most obvious ele-ment: color. Create a list of not only wall color but also floor color and tones and trim colors (stained or

A corner niche of the guest bedroom fea-tures European furniture, a concrete mantel that was found for $350, and an Aubusson rug over antique Southern pine finished floors.

(**Left**) A kitchen corner view that provides a detailed look at the Zodiac line of countertops from Corian and a closer look at the Willow Bough wallpaper reproduced in the Arts and Crafts style by Sanderson & Sons. (**Right**) The kitchen backsplash shows the interesting combination of materials, including tumble marble, cherry trim, and Arthur Sanderson & Sons wallpaper.

painted in contrasting color). Make a similar list for each element of the room, including ceilings, lighting, window treatments, and furnishings. Dissecting will help you pull it all together and understand the designer's thought process. Writing will help you clarify what you really want; think of your written plans as the road map that will take you where you want to go with your project.

FOCUS ON THE BIG PICTURE

Along with color, architectural elements are essential when planning a room's overall style. Whether it is a fireplace mantel, built-in shelving, or large furniture pieces, these elements will set the tone for the rest of the room. Items of this magnitude should be the focus of attention because of their permanence and their cost. Pay closer attention to what you may have to live with for many years than what may be easily changed or replaced.

DON'T FORGET LIGHTING AND FIXTURES

Chandeliers and sconces are the first elements that will be seen upon entering a room because the eye is attracted to light. Therefore, these elements should be treated as room jewelry, and consumers should buy the Tiffany or Cartier version. If at all possible, make a statement with quality and design when choosing these items.

MAKE A SHOPPING LIST

Once the key elements have been noted, start making a list of all the

pieces needed to complete the look. Take the list whenever you are shopping and refer to both the list and your photos when purchasing items for the room. Professionals use this method 90 percent of the time when designing. In addition to keeping your wants and needs in focus, a shopping list will give you a better idea of budget and help you prioritize what is urgent and what can wait.

STAY OPEN TO SURPRISES

Even when you have a very clear visual image of the rooms you want to create, staying open to surprising finds can help to make the process more fun. Interesting and unusual accessories found in thrift stores or at tag sales may inspire a change in direction, but don't let this keep you away from items you are drawn to. Decorating surprises can also take the form of unusual combinations, and again the juxtaposition of new and old can be fun. Trust your eye when creating such juxtapositions: is there something in the form that connects them? Is there a color that ties the two accessories together? Or is there a fond memory that makes your grandmother's samplers look good next to a family photo?

(Left) The ceiling fixture in the master bathroom is an antique French bronze-and-rock crystal chandelier and is a great example of room jewelry. (Right) This view of the master bath shows Kohler's beautiful soaking tub. Walls are clad in Arts and Crafts paneling installed at the factory with detailed millwork that is indicative of stick-built construction. The rich black/green Pratt & Lambert paint suggests the color of a European garden room, and the elaborate moldings from Style Solutions allow for a seamless transition between 9-foot walls and a tented ceiling.

"THE GOAL FOR THIS PROJECT WAS TO IMPLEMENT CHANGES IN MODULAR DESIGN THAT WOULD IMPROVE BOTH THE REALITY AND THE IMAGE OF MODULAR CONSTRUCTION. THE OUTCOME AND SUCCESS OF PUTTING A DESIGNER'S EYE ON THIS MODEL OF BUILDING HAS RAISED THE BAR FOR THE MODULAR INDUSTRY."

A view of the kitchen from the dining room shows the interesting archway detail between the two rooms—an important architectural detail from the earlier catalog homes. This view also shows the combination of wood and paint finishes on the cabinets, with the beautiful green center cabinets breaking up the extended area of wood finish.

The learning curve attached to this project was enormous, but like any dream that is realized or challenge that is successfully met, it was extremely fulfilling as well. Anyone who has built a house will tell you there are moments of frustration that leave you questioning both your sanity and your very desire to continue. In this case, all of the headaches came to life when the on-site finish work was set to begin. The slow process of completion seemed amplified by how quickly the bulk of the house had been assembled at the factory. Now there were weather delays, unexpected cost overruns, difficulty with supervision of on-site tradesmen, and the added pressure of having to meet a television production schedule. A project of this nature and scope can be equal to a college education: one has to pay to learn, and this venture would prove to be an Ivy League endeavor.

Because of the level of finish desired for the high-style look of the Berkshire model, both interior and exterior completion took much longer than originally planned for—but in some ways, this was to be expected. There are some things that can expedite the process of

finish work; one is timing the modular set so completion of exterior work can be accomplished before weather becomes a problem. Consumers who are interested in speed could be living in a modular house shortly after its assembly; and this is especially true for do-it-yourselfers who want to move in and complete such things as painting and papering on their own. The focal point here was not speed, however, but accuracy: precise attention to every detail and layering on of nuances and designer touches.

One difficulty that was unforeseen was that the home was under construction in an area where craft

(**Left**) The stairway has been built and installed by a master craftsman at the factory. On-site, the pieces will be joined to provide access to the second floor and finishing will be completed.
(**Right**) Members of the set crew watch as the second-floor section is moved into place.

(**Left**) Subcontractors install wood flooring at the marriage wall once the units have been set in place. The majority of the floor installation is completed at the factory; minor on-site finishing is required where one unit meets another.

(**Opposite Page Left**) The kitchen with cabinets, island, and factory-installed countertops still must be papered and painted. Detailed trim will be added to the cabinetry to create an Arts and Crafts finish detail.

(**Opposite Page Right**) The master bedroom is used as a storage area as on-site finish work progresses. All floors are protected by sheets of thin particle board to prevent damage to newly installed floors.

and tradesmen were much more expensive than originally thought—even higher, in some cases, than the New York metropolitan area. The impact on the bottom line was becoming so pronounced that new estimates were required for some installation work; this slowed the project somewhat but is perhaps something that can be avoided by getting several estimates in the pre-planning stage. The modular company can also give you ballpark estimates of some work; that makes it easier to raise questions when subcontractors begin supplying their approximation of costs. Keep in mind that the modular company is also available to assist on-site crewmen with questions that may arise as work proceeds.

A project of this nature can also be viewed as something like the birth of a child. The romance surrounding the creation of an heir is wonderful, but whether the pregnancy is easy or difficult, by the eighth or ninth month your excitement has lessened and your patience is waning. The birth is extremely painful; but once that is over, a beautiful bundle of joy remains, and the pain and anxiety are forgotten. This scenario is very similar to the building process. As the project nears completion, your enthusiasm diminishes, and your only hope is to just get it done. But once the final project is complete, in some

MODULAR MINUTIAE: FUTURE

· Visual impact that is indistinguish-
  able from conventional site-built
· New structural processes and materials, including block concrete, pre-
  cast concrete, and steel
· Use of nontraditional and recycled
  products to increase affordability
  and durability
· Better factory technology to accommodate innovation in design
· Creative integration of prefabrication
  and conventional building
· Homes that blend with the architectural personality of existing
  neighborhoods

(Source: U.S. Department of Housing at
www.hud.gov)

miraculous way the pain, aggravation, and lost sweat are forgotten, and the focus is on the reason you went through the project in the first place: a beautiful creation.

The goal for this project was to implement changes in modular design that would improve both the reality and the image of modular construction. The outcome and success of putting a designer's eye on this model of building has raised the bar for the modular industry. Public response has been positive, and there has been a strong interest in finding out more about how this house was created and styled. The Berkshire construction project appeared on a national TV show, and

(**Opposite Page Left**) This exterior rear view shows the dining room wing and deck. Deck materials from Weyerhaeuser are made from recycled products and are a low-maintenance option requiring no stain or finish. (**Opposite Page Right**) View of the master bathroom: a generous soaking tub is flanked by Kohler vanities. (**Left**) Swag crown molding from Style Solutions awaits installation. The moldings are available in many designs and are pre-finished. Pre-cut corners mean no complicated mitering and easy installation.

(Left) A detail of the bungalow-style colonnade showing a pergola with detailed ends. (Right) This cabinet in the master bath was meant to look like it was original to a bungalow house. It was actually purchased from Rejuvenation, a company known for cabinet, light fixture, and hardware reproductions. The sconces are in the same style and are another inexpensive Arts and Crafts detail from Hampton Bay.

the response from viewers has been enormous, with calls and inquiries to the modular company that were directly traceable to the TV show. The show had a positive message about the modular industry, and viewers have been moved to inquire about an industry that they may have had little interest in before. The recurring comment is that they had no idea that modular construction could be so beautiful. As such, there is still much to be done to erase the cookie-cutter reputation that seems so strongly held.

Nearly ten years ago, the Manufactured Housing Industry declared 1995–2005 as the "Decade of Manufactured Housing." In doing so, they affirmed a commitment not only to building a brighter future for the industry but also to changing the errors and omissions of the past. Consumers who demand better quality and who are involved in all aspects of the building process have helped immeasurably. Not so long ago, the delivery of a modular home would inspire onlookers to remark, "There

goes the neighborhood." This attitude is slowly being replaced with a new curiosity about the possibilities of modular construction, particularly as it takes on new forms, design, and materials. As with the two projects discussed here, the neighbors now may well remark, "This is a modular?"

It will be interesting to see where modular construction will be heading in the next ten to fifteen years. Technology and innovation will help to perfect the building of these homes, and improved transportation will allow for delivery of more-complex parts. One can only hope that the aesthetic level will

Completed exterior settings showcase the wonderful use of texture, tones, and color. All of the elements that would typically be found on a period bungalow are captured here.

keep up with the technical innovations and that the affordability factor will not be lost as the overall visual impact is enhanced. The modular industry itself has set several goals for the next decade, including the use of recycled products and other nontraditional building materials, the further integration of factory and site-built, and the continued focus on quality.

Ralph Waldo Emerson said, "We ascribe beauty to that which is simple; which has no superfluous parts; which exactly answers its end; which stands related to all things; which is the mean of many extremes." Surely then, beauty can be ascribed to this home (and to its Pennsylvania cousin). The Berkshire model is a sanctuary that finds kinship with both the New England landscape and the traditions of American design; the Simplex model is proof enough that cost reductions can make the hope of home ownership available to a new generation of dreamers.

(**Right**) The finished front elevation of the house. The goal was to create the appearance of a home that had been there for many years. The wings appear as if they were added years after the original Cape-style main house. Different materials were used to add visual interest and a sense of old-world charm.

RESOURCES

Art/Antiques

Michael Buchanan Style Collection
New York, NY
570-296-9984
An eclectic array of soft furnishings, lighting, hardware, art, and antiques chosen by Michael with an eye for an old-world or European aesthetic

Cabinetry

Merillat
Detroit, MI
517-263-0771
www.merillat.com
Beautiful cabinetry with many designer details and the look of hand finishing

Columns

Chadsworth Columns
Wilmington, NC
800-265-8667
www.columns.com
Beautifully proportioned columns and pilasters; bungalow line offers perfect craftsman detail

Drapery

Calico Corners
Kennett Square, PA
800-213-6366
www.calicocorners.com
Fantastic retail source for do-it-yourself decorators; decorating made easy and affordable; highly recommended whether you are working with or without a designer

Exterior Decking

Weyerhaeuser
Federal Way, WA
800-525-5440
www.weyerhaeuser.com
A great alternative to pressure-treated wood

Fireplace Inserts

CFM Specialty Home Products
Mississauga, ON, Canada
905-670-7777
www.vermontcastings.com
Inventive solution for gas fireplace inserts with a focus on pleasing designs

Flooring/Interior

Lumber Liquidators
Colonial Heights, VA
1-800-FLOORING
www.lumberliquidators.com
Excellent source for natural wood flooring; easily accessible to buying public

Foundation

Superior Walls
New Holland, PA
800-452-9255
www.superiorwalls.com
Excellent watertight foundation system that keeps the basement water-free and warm, with insulation as part of the exterior walls

Furniture

Avery Boardman
New York, NY
800-501-4850
www.averyboardman.com
Offered through the designer trade; superb resource for upholstery, especially sleep sofas and custom beds

Price Pfister
Foothill Ranch, CA
800-732-8238
www.pricepfister.com
Large selection of styles and finishes available to retail buyers

Baker Furniture for Kohler Interiors
Kohler, WI
800-59-BAKER
www.kohlerinteriors.com

Calico Corners
Kennett Square, PA
800-213-6366
www.calicocorners.com
First-rate source for affordable, custom upholstery

McGuire Furniture for Kohler Interiors
Kohler, WI
800-662-4847
www.kohlerinteriors.com

Hardware

Emtek Products Inc.
City of Industry, CA
800-356-2741
www.emtek.com
Attractive and affordable
high-end hardware

Lighting/Ceiling Fans

Rejuvenation
Portland, OR
888-401-1900
www.rejuvenation.com
Wonderful selection of
period-style fixtures and
hardware

The Home Depot
Nationwide
www.homedepot.com

Mantels

Chesney's, Inc.
New York, NY
866-840-0609
www.chesneys-usa.com
One of the best sources for
authentic, period reproduction European fireplace
mantels; beautiful stones,
gorgeous detailing, easy to
work with

Paint

Pratt and Lambert
Buffalo, NY
800-289-7728
www.prattandlambert.com

Benjamin Moore
Montvale, NJ
800-344-0400
www.benjaminmoore.com

The following sources
were used for accents,
accessories, objects, and
ornaments:

The TJX Companies Inc.
TJ Maxx, HomeGoods,
Marshalls
Framingham, MA
508-390-1000
www.tjx.com

Bombay Company
Fort Worth, TX
888-2BOMBAY
www.bombaycompany.com

Visual Comfort
Houston, TX
713-686-5999
www.visualcomfort.com

Pottery Barn
Nationwide
888-779-5176
www.potterybarn.com

Crate & Barrel
Nationwide/Online
800-967-6696
www.crateandbarrel.com

The Home Depot
Nationwide
www.homedepot.com

**Lowe's Home Improvement
Centers**
Nationwide
www.lowes.com

Photography

Franklin & Esther Schmidt
888-987-8410
www.feschmidtphotog-
raphy.com

Plumbing/Fixtures

Kohler Plumbing
Kohler, WI
800-456-4537
www.kohler.com
Fine-looking products;
readily accessible to the
buying public

American Standard
Piscataway, NJ
800-442-1902
www.americanstandard.com
Great classic pedestal sinks
and toilets

Moen
North Olmstead, OH
800-BUY-MOEN
www.moen.com
Innovative design and finishes
that don't break the bank

Roofing

Enviroshake
Chatham, ON, Canada
866-423-3302
www.enviroshake.com
Environmentally friendly
company, makes amazing
simulated cedar shakes
from recycled tires

Shutters/Window Boxes

Michael Buchanan Style Collection
New York, NY
570-296-9984
Custom-designed and built shutters and window boxes

Siding

Cedar Valley Shingles
Hollister, CA
800-521-9523
www.cedar-valley.com
Terrific natural cedar shingles in handcrafted panels that are easily installed

Stone Cladding

Owens Corning Cultured Stone
Napa, CA
800-255-1727
www.culturedstone.com
Pre-cast stone veneer; wonderful textures, shapes, and colors will fool even the expert's eye

Switches

Lutron
Coopersburg, PA
888-LUTRON1
www.lutron.com

Tile/Stone

Ann Sacks
New York, NY
212-529-2800
www.annsacks.com
Primarily offered through the designer trade but can be purchased retail; terrific source for the most current styles, colors, and trends in stone and tile

Dal-Tile Corporation
Dallas, TX
214-398-1411
www.daltile.com
High-style tiles that will withstand high use; wide variety to choose from

Zodiac by Corian
Division of DuPont
Wilmington, DE
800-426-7426
www.corian.com
Interesting alternative to natural stone

Trim Details

Style Solutions
Archold, OH
800-446-3040
www.stylesolutionsinc.com
Exquisite simulated-plaster moldings; gorgeous detail in all their products

Wallpaper

Sanderson & Sons Ltd.
William Morris Collection
New York, NY
212-319-7220

Windows/Doors

Pella
Pella, IA
641-621-1000
www.pella.com
Wide selection of window and door styles

Kolbe & Kolbe Millwork Co., Inc.
Wausau, WI
800-477-8656
www.kolbeandkolbe.com
Affordable, custom-quality windows and doors with top-notch details and palette

Kichler
Cleveland, OH
800-875-4216
www.kichler.com

Lowe's Home Improvement Centers
Nationwide
www.lowes.com